The Analyst

A Discourse addressed to an Infidel Mathematician

Wherein
It is examined whether the Object, Principles, and
Inferences of the modern Analysis are more distinctly
conceived, or more evidently deduced, than Religious
Mysteries and Points of Faith.

by

George Berkeley

Table of Contents

10.   Implicit Deference of Mathematical-men for the great Author of Fluxions. Their earnestness rather to go on fast and far, than to set out warily and see their way distinctly.

11.   Momentums difficult to comprehend. No middle Quantity to be admitted between a finite Quantity and nothing, without admitting Infinitesimals.

12.   The Fluxion of any Power of a flowing Quantity. Lemma premised in order to examine the method for finding such Fluxion.

13.   The rule for the Fluxions of Powers attained by unfair reasoning.

14.   The aforesaid reasoning farther unfolded, and shew'd to be illogical.

15.   No true Conclusion to be justly drawn by direct consequence from inconsistent Suppositions. The same Rules of right reason to be observed, whether Men argue in Symbols or in Words.

16.   An Hypothesis being destroyed, no consequence of such Hypothesis to be retained.

17.   Hard to distinguish between evanescent Increments and infinitesimal Differences. Fluxions placed in various Lights. The great Author, it seems, not satisfied with his own Notions.

18.   Quantities infinitely small supposed and rejected by Leibnitz and his Followers. No Quantity, according to them, greater or smaller for the Addition or Subduction of its Infinitesimal.

19.   Conclusions to be proved by the Principles, and not Principles by the Conclusions.

20.   The Geometrical Analyst considered as a Logician; and his Discoveries, not in themselves, but as derived from such Principles and by such Inferences.

21.   A Tangent drawn to the Parabola according to the calculus differentialis. Truth shewn to be the result of error, and how.

22.   By virtue of a twofold mistake Analysts arrive at Truth, but not at Science: ignorant how they come at their own Conclusions.

23.   The Conclusion never evident or accurate, in virtue of obscure or inaccurate Premises. Finite Quantities might be rejected as well as Infinitesimals.

24.   The foregoing Doctrine farther illustrated.

25.   Sundry Observations thereupon.

26.   Ordinate found from the Area by means of evanescent Increments.

27.   In the foregoing Case the supposed evanescent Increment is really a finite Quantity, destroyed by an equal Quantity with an opposite Sign.

28.   The foregoing Case put generally. Algebraical Expressions compared with Geometrical Quantities.

29.   Correspondent Quantities Algebraical and Geometrical equated. The analysis shewed not to obtain in Infinitesimals, but it must also obtain in finite Quantities.

30.   The getting rid of Quantities by the received Principles, whether of Fluxions or of Differences, neither good Geometry nor good Logic. Fluxions or Velocities, why introduced.

31.   Velocities not to be abstracted from Time and Space: Nor their Proportions to be investigated or considered exclusively of Time and Space.

32.   Difficult and obscure Points constitute the Principles of the modern Analysis, and are the Foundation on which it is built.

33.   The rational Faculties whether improved by such obscure Analytics.

34.   By what inconceivable Steps finite lines are found proportional to Fluxions. Mathematical Infidels strain at a Gnat and swallow a Camel.

35.   Fluxions or Infinitesimals not to be avoided on the received Principles. Nice Abstractions and Geometrical Metaphysics.

36.   Velocities of nascent or evanescent Quantities, whether in reality understood and signified by finite Lines and Species.

37.   Signs or Exponents obvious; but Fluxions themselves not so.

38.   Fluxions, whether the Velocities with which infinitesimal Differences are generated?

39.   Fluxions of Fluxions or second Fluxions, whether to be conceived as Velocities of Velocities, or rather as Velocities of the second nascent Increments?

40.   Fluxions considered, sometimes in one Sense, sometimes in another: One while in themselves, another in their Exponents: Hence Confusion and Obscurity.

41.   Isochronal Increments, whether finite or nascent, proportional to their respective Velocities.

42.   Time supposed to be divided into Moments: Increments generated in those Moments: And Velocities proportional to those Increments.

43.   Fluxions, second, third, fourth, &c. what they are, how obtained, and how represented. What Idea of Velocity in a Moment of Time and Point of Space.

44.   Fluxions of all Orders inconceivable.

45.   Signs or Exponents confounded with the Fluxions.

46.   Series of Expressions or of Notes easily contrived. Whether a Series, of mere Velocities, or of mere nascent Increments, corresponding thereunto, be as easily conceived?

47.   Celerities dismissed, and instead thereof Ordinates and Areas introduced. Analogies and Expressions useful in the modern Quadratures, may yet be useless for enabling us to conceive Fluxions. No right to apply the Rules without knowledge of the Principles.

48.   Metaphysics of modern Analysts most incomprehensible.

49.   Analysts employ'd about notional shadowy Entities. Their Logics as exceptionable as their Metaphysics.

50.   Occasion of this Address. Conclusion. Queries.

The Analyst

I. Though I am a Stranger to your Person, yet I am not, Sir, a Stranger to the Reputation you have acquired, in that branch of Learning which hath been your peculiar Study; nor to the Authority that you therefore assume in things foreign to your Profession, nor to the Abuse that you, and too many more of the like Character, are known to make of such undue Authority, to the misleading of unwary Persons in matters of the highest Concernment, and whereof your mathematical Knowledge can by no means qualify you to be a competent Judge. Equity indeed and good Sense would incline one to disregard the Judgment of Men, in Points which they have not considered or examined. But several who make the loudest Claim to those Qualities, do, nevertheless, the very thing they would seem to despise, clothing themselves in the Livery of other Mens Opinions, and putting on a general deference for the Judgment of you, Gentlemen, who are presumed to be of all Men the greatest Masters of Reason, to be most conversant about distinct Ideas, and never to take things on trust, but always clearly to see your way, as Men whose constant Employment is the deducing Truth by the justest inference from the most evident Principles. With this bias on their Minds, they submit to your Decisions where you have no right to decide. And that this is one short way of making Infidels I am credibly informed.

II. Whereas then it is supposed, that you apprehend more distinctly, consider more closely, infer more justly, conclude more accurately than other Men, and that you are therefore less religious because more judicious, I shall claim the privilege of a Free-Thinker; and take the Liberty to inquire into the Object, Principles, and Method of Demonstration admitted by the Mathematicians of the present Age, with the same freedom that you presume to treat the Principles and Mysteries of Religion; to the end, that all Men may see what right you have to lead, or what Encouragement others have to follow you. It hath been an old remark that Geometry is an excellent Logic. And it must be owned, that when the Definitions are clear; when the Postulata cannot be refused, nor the Axioms denied; when from the distinct Contemplation and Comparison of Figures, their Properties are derived, by a perpetual well-connected chain of Consequences, the Objects being still kept in view, and the attention ever fixed upon them; there is acquired a habit of reasoning, close and exact and methodical: which habit strengthens and sharpens the Mind, and being transferred to other Subjects, is of general use in the inquiry after Truth. But how far this is the case of our Geometrical Analysts, it may be worth while to consider.

III. The Method of Fluxions is the general Key, by help whereof the modern Mathematicians unlock the secrets of Geometry, and consequently of Nature. And as it is that which hath enabled them so remarkably to outgo the Ancients in discovering Theorems and solving Problems, the exercise and application thereof is become the main, if not sole, employment of all those who in this Age pass for profound Geometers. But whether this Method be clear or obscure, consistent or repugnant, demonstrative or precarious, as I shall inquire with the utmost impartiality, so I submit my inquiry to your own Judgment, and that of every candid Reader. Lines are supposed to be generated [NOTE: Introd. ad Quadraturam Curvarum.] by the motion of Points, Planes by the motion of Lines, and Solids by the motion of Planes. And whereas Quantities generated in equal times are greater or lesser, according to the greater or lesser Velocity, wherewith they increase and are generated, a Method hath been found to determine Quantities from the Velocities of their generating Motions. And such Velocities are called Fluxions: and the Quantities generated are called flowing Quantities. These Fluxions are said to be nearly as the Increments of the flowing Quantities, generated in the least equal Particles of time; and to be accurately in the first Proportion of the nascent, or in the last of the evanescent, Increments. Sometimes, instead of Velocities, the momentaneous Increments or Decrements of undetermined flowing Quantities are considered, under the Appellation of Moments.

IV. By Moments we are not to understand finite Particles. These are said not to be Moments, but Quantities generated from Moments, which last are only the nascent Principles of finite Quantities. It is said, that the minutest Errors are not to be neglected in Mathematics: that the Fluxions are Celerities, not proportional to the finite Increments though ever so small; but only to the Moments or nascent Increments, whereof the Proportion alone, and not the Magnitude, is considered. And of the aforesaid Fluxions there be other Fluxions, which Fluxions of Fluxions are called second Fluxions. And the Fluxions of these second Fluxions are called third Fluxions: and so on, fourth, fifth, sixth, &c. ad infinitum. Now as our Sense is strained and puzzled with the perception of Objects extremely minute, even so the Imagination, which Faculty derives from Sense, is very much strained and puzzled to frame clear Ideas of the least Particles of time, or the least Increments generated therein: and much more so to comprehend the Moments, or those Increments of the flowing Quantities in *statu nascenti*, in their very first origin or beginning to exist, before they become finite Particles. And it seems still more difficult, to conceive the abstracted Velocities of such nascent imperfect Entities. But the Velocities of the Velocities, the second, third, fourth, and fifth Velocities, &c. exceed, if I mistake not, all Humane Understanding. The further the Mind analyseth and pursueth these fugitive Ideas, the more it is lost and bewildered; the Objects, at first fleeting and minute, soon vanishing out of sight. Certainly in any Sense a second or third Fluxion seems an obscure Mystery. The incipient Celerity of an incipient Celerity, the nascent Augment of a nascent Augment, *i. e.* of a thing which hath no Magnitude: Take it in which light you please, the clear Conception of it will, if I mistake not, be found impossible, whether it be so or no I appeal to the trial of every thinking Reader. And if a second Fluxion be inconceivable, what are we to think of third, fourth, fifth Fluxions, and so onward without end?

V. The foreign Mathematicians are supposed by some, even of our own, to proceed in a manner, less accurate perhaps and geometrical, yet more intelligible. Instead of flowing Quantities and their Fluxions, they consider the variable finite Quantities, as increasing or diminishing by the continual Addition or Subduction of infinitely small Quantities. Instead of the Velocities wherewith Increments are generated, they consider the Increments or Decrements themselves, which they call Differences, and which are supposed to be infinitely small. The Difference of a Line is an infinitely little Line; of a Plane an infinitely little Plane. They suppose finite Quantities to consist of Parts infinitely little, and Curves to be Polygons, whereof the Sides are infinitely little, which by the Angles they make one with another determine the Curvity of the Line. Now to conceive a Quantity infinitely small, that is, infinitely less than any sensible or imaginable Quantity, or any the least finite Magnitude, is, I confess, above my Capacity. But to conceive a Part of such infinitely small Quantity, that shall be still infinitely less than it, and consequently though multiply'd infinitely shall never equal the minutest finite Quantity, is, I suspect, an infinite Difficulty to any Man whatsoever; and will be allowed such by those who candidly say what they think; provided they really think and reflect, and do not take things upon trust.

VI. And yet in the *calculus differentialis*, which Method serves to all the same Intents and Ends with that of Fluxions, our modern Analysts are not content to consider only the Differences of finite Quantities: they also consider the Differences of those Differences, and the Differences of the Differences of the first Differences. And so on *ad infinitum*. That is, they consider Quantities infinitely less than the least discernible Quantity; and others infinitely less than those infinitely small ones; and still others infinitely less than the preceding Infinitesimals, and so on without end or limit. Insomuch that we are to admit an infinite succession of Infinitesimals, each infinitely less than the foregoing, and infinitely greater than the following. As there are first, second, third, fourth, fifth &c. Fluxions, so there are Differences, first, second, third fourth, &c. in an infinite Progression towards nothing, which you still approach and never arrive at. And (which is most strange) although you should take a Million of Millions of these Infinitesimals, each whereof is supposed infinitely greater than some other real Magnitude, and add them to the least given Quantity, it shall be never the bigger. For this is one of the modest *postulata* of our modern Mathematicians, and is a Corner-stone or Ground-work of their Speculations.

VII. All these Points, I say, are supposed and believed by certain rigorous Exactors of Evidence in Religion, Men who pretend to believe no further than they can see. That Men, who have been conversant only about clear Points, should with difficulty admit obscure ones might not seem altogether unaccountable. But he who can digest a second or third Fluxion, a second or third Difference, need not, methinks, be squeamish about any Point in Divinity. There is a natural Presumption that Mens Faculties are made alike. It is on this Supposition that they attempt to argue and convince one another. What, therefore, shall appear evidently impossible and repugnant to one, may be presumed the same to another. But with what appearance of Reason shall any Man presume to say, that Mysteries may not be Objects of Faith, at the same time that he himself admits such obscure Mysteries to be the Object of Science?

VIII. It must indeed be acknowledged, the modern Mathematicians do not consider these Points as Mysteries, but as clearly conceived and mastered by their comprehensive Minds. They scruple not to say, that by the help of these new Analytics they can penetrate into Infinity it self: That they can even extend their Views beyond Infinity: that their Art comprehends not only

Infinite, but Infinite of Infinite (as they express it) or an Infinity of Infinites. But, notwithstanding all these Assertions and Pretensions, it may be justly questioned whether, as other Men in other Inquiries are often deceived by Words or Terms, so they likewise are not wonderfully deceived and deluded by their own peculiar Signs, Symbols, or Species. Nothing is easier than to devise Expressions or Notations for Fluxions and Infinitesimals of the first, second, third, fourth, and subsequent Orders, proceeding in the same regular form without end or limit $\dot{x}$. $\ddot{x}$. $\dddot{x}$. $\ddddot{x}$. &c. or dx. ddx. $dddx$. $ddddx$. &c. These Expressions indeed are clear and distinct, and the Mind finds no difficulty in conceiving them to be continued beyond any assignable Bounds. But if we remove the Veil and look underneath, if laying aside the Expressions we set ourselves attentively to consider the things themselves, which are supposed to be expressed or marked thereby, we shall discover much Emptiness, Darkness, and Confusion; nay, if I mistake not, direct Impossibilities and Contradictions. Whether this be the case or no, every thinking Reader is intreated to examine and judge for himself.

IX. Having considered the Object, I proceed to consider the Principles of this new Analysis by Momentums, Fluxions, or Infinitesimals; wherein if it shall appear that your capital Points, upon which the rest are supposed to depend, include Error and false Reasoning; it will then follow that you, who are at a loss to conduct your selves, cannot with any decency set up for guides to other Men. The main Point in the method of Fluxions is to obtain the Fluxion or Momentum of the Rectangle or Product of two indeterminate Quantities. Inasmuch as from thence are derived Rules for obtaining the Fluxions of all other Products and Powers; be the Coefficients or the Indexes what they will, integers or fractions, rational or surd. Now this fundamental Point one would think should be very clearly made out, considering how much is built upon it, and that its Influence extends throughout the whole Analysis. But let the Reader judge. This is given for Demonstration. [NOTE: Naturalis Philosophiæ principia mathematica, 1. 2. lem. 2.] Suppose the Product or Rectangle AB increased by continual Motion: and that the momentaneous Increments of the Sides A and B are a and b. When the Sides A and B were deficient, or lesser by one half of their Moments, the Rectangle was

$$\overline{A - \tfrac{1}{2}a} \times \overline{B - \tfrac{1}{2}b},$$

i. e.,

$$AB - \tfrac{1}{2}aB - \tfrac{1}{2}bA + \tfrac{1}{4}ab.$$

And as soon as the Sides A and B are increased by the other two halves of their Moments, the Rectangle becomes

$$\overline{A + \tfrac{1}{2}a} \times \overline{B + \tfrac{1}{2}b}$$

or

$$AB + \tfrac{1}{2}aB + \tfrac{1}{2}bA + \tfrac{1}{4}ab.$$

From the latter Rectangle subduct the former, and the remaining Difference will be $aB + bA$. Therefore the Increment of the Rectangle generated by the intire Increments a and b is $aB + bA$. Q.E.D. But it is plain that the direct and true Method to obtain the Moment or Increment of the Rectangle AB, is to take the Sides as increased by their whole Increments, and so multiply them together, $A + a$ by $B + b$, the Product whereof $AB + aB + bA + ab$ is the augmented Rectangle; whence if we subduct AB, the Remainder $aB + bA + ab$ will be the true Increment of the Rectangle, exceeding that which was obtained by the former illegitimate and indirect Method by the Quantity ab. And this holds universally be the Quantities a and b what they will, big or little, Finite or Infinitesimal, Increments, Moments, or Velocities. Nor will it avail to say that *ab* is a Quantity exceeding small: Since we are told that *in rebus mathematicis errores quàm minimi non sunt contemnendi.* [NOTE: Introd. ad Quadraturam Curvarum.]

X. Such reasoning as this for Demonstration, nothing but the obscurity of the Subject could have encouraged or induced the great Author of the Fluxionary Method to put upon his Followers, and nothing but an implicit deference to Authority could move them to admit. The Case indeed is difficult. There can be nothing done till you have got rid of the Quantity *ab*. In order to this the Notion of Fluxions is shifted: it is placed in various Lights: Points which should be as clear as first Principles are puzzled; and Terms which should be steadily used are ambiguous. But notwithstanding all this address and skill the point of getting rid of *ab* cannot be obtained by legitimate reasoning. If a Man by Methods, not geometrical or demonstrative, shall have satisfied himself of the usefulness of certain Rules; which he afterwards shall propose to his Disciples for undoubted Truths; which he undertakes to demonstrate in a subtile manner, and by the help of nice and intricate Notions; it is not hard to conceive that such his Disciples may, to save themselves the trouble of thinking, be inclined to confound the usefulness of a Rule with the certainty of a Truth, and accept the one for the other; especially if they are Men accustomed rather to compute than to think; earnest rather to go on fast and far, than solicitous to set out warily and see their way distinctly.

XI. The Points or meer Limits of nascent Lines are undoubtedly equal, as having no more magnitude one than another, a Limit as such being no Quantity. If by a Momentum you mean more than the very initial Limit, it must be either a finite Quantity or an Infinitesimal. But all finite Quantities are expressly excluded from the Notion of a Momentum. Therefore the Momentum must be an Infinitesimal. And indeed, though much Artifice hath been employ'd to escape or avoid the admission of Quantities infinitely small, yet it seems ineffectual. For ought I see, you can admit no Quantity as a Medium between a finite Quantity and nothing, without admitting Infinitesimals. An Increment generated in a finite Particle of Time, is it self a finite Particle; and cannot therefore be a Momentum. You must therefore take an Infinitesimal Part of Time wherein to generate your Momentum. It is said, the Magnitude of Moments is not considered: And yet these same Moments are supposed to be divided into Parts. This is not easy to conceive, no more than it is why we should take Quantities less than A and B in order to obtain the Increment of AB, of which proceeding it must be owned the final Cause or Motive is very obvious; but it is not so obvious or easy to explain a just and legitimate Reason for it, or shew it to be Geometrical.

XII. From the foregoing Principle so demonstrated, the general Rule for finding the Fluxion of any Power of a flowing Quantity is derived. [NOTE: Philosophiæ naturalis principia Mathematica, lib. 2. lem. 2.] But, as there seems to have been some inward Scruple or Consciousness of defect in the foregoing Demonstration, and as this finding the Fluxion of a given Power is a Point of primary Importance, it hath therefore been judged proper to demonstrate the same in a different manner independent of the foregoing Demonstration. But whether this other Method be more legitimate and conclusive than the former, I proceed now to examine; and in order thereto shall premise the following Lemma. "If with a View to demonstrate any Proposition, a certain Point is supposed, by virtue of which certain other Points are attained; and such supposed Point be it self afterwards destroyed or rejected by a contrary Supposition; in that case, all the other Points, attained thereby and consequent thereupon, must also be destroyed and rejected, so as from thence forward to be no more supposed or applied in the Demonstration." This is so plain as to need no Proof.

XIII. Now the other Method of obtaining a Rule to find the Fluxion of any Power is as follows. Let the Quantity x flow uniformly, and be it proposed to find the Fluxion of x^n. In the same time that x by flowing becomes $x + o$, the Power x^n becomes $\overline{x + o}\,|^n$, i. e. by the Method of infinite Series

$$x^n + nox^{n-1} + \frac{nn - n}{2}\,oox^{n-2} + \&c.$$

and the Increments

$$o \text{ and } nox^{n-1} + \frac{nn - n}{2}\,oox^{n-2} + \&c.$$

are to one another as

$$1 \text{ to } nx^{n-1} + \frac{nn - n}{2}\,ox^{n-2} + \&c.$$

Let now the Increments vanish, and their last Proportion will be 1 to nx^{n-1}. But it should seem that this reasoning is not fair or conclusive. For when it is said, let the Increments vanish, i. e. let the Increments be nothing, or let there be no Increments, the former Supposition that the Increments were something, or that there were Increments, is destroyed, and yet a Consequence of that Supposition, i. e. an Expression got by virtue thereof, is retained. Which, by the foregoing Lemma, is a false way of reasoning. Certainly when we suppose the Increments to vanish, we must suppose their Proportions, their Expressions, and every thing else derived from the Supposition of their Existence to vanish with them.

XIV. To make this Point plainer, I shall unfold the reasoning, and propose it in a fuller light to your View. It amounts therefore to this, or may in other Words be thus expressed. I suppose that the Quantity x flows, and by flowing is increased, and its

Increment I call o, so that by flowing it becomes $x + o$. And as x increaseth, it follows that every Power of x is likewise increased in a due Proportion. Therefore as x becomes $x + o$, x^n will become $\overline{x + o}^n$: that is, according to the Method of infinite Series,

$$x^n + nox^{n-1} + \frac{nn - n}{2} oox^{n-2} + \&c.$$

And if from the two augmented Quantities we subduct the Root and the Power respectively, we shall have remaining the two Increments, to wit,

$$o \text{ and } nox^{n-1} + \frac{nn - n}{2} oox^{n-2} + \&c.$$

which Increments, being both divided by the common Divisor o, yield the Quotients

$$1 \text{ and } nx^{n-1} + \frac{nn - n}{2} ox^{n-2} + \&c.$$

which are therefore Exponents of the Ratio of the Increments. Hitherto I have supposed that x flows, that x hath a real Increment, that o is something. And I have proceeded all along on that Supposition, without which I should not have been able to have made so much as one single Step. From that Supposition it is that I get at the Increment of x^n, that I am able to compare it with the Increment of x, and that I find the Proportion between the two Increments. I now beg leave to make a new Supposition contrary to the first, *i. e.* I will suppose that there is no Increment of x, or that o is nothing; which second Supposition destroys my first, and is inconsistent with it, and therefore with every thing that supposeth it. I do nevertheless beg leave to retain nx^{n-1}, which is an Expression obtained in virtue of my first Supposition, which necessarily presupposeth such Supposition, and which could not be obtained without it: All which seems a most inconsistent way of arguing, and such as would not be allowed of in Divinity.

XV. Nothing is plainer than that no just Conclusion can be directly drawn from two inconsistent Suppositions. You may indeed suppose any thing possible: But afterwards you may not suppose any thing that destroys what you first supposed. Or if you do, you must begin *de novo*. If therefore you suppose that the Augments vanish, *i. e.* that there are no Augments, you are to begin again, and see what follows from such Supposition. But nothing will follow to your purpose. You cannot by that means ever arrive at your Conclusion, or succeed in, what is called by the celebrated Author, the Investigation of the first or last Proportions of nascent and evanescent Quantities, by instituting the Analysis in finite ones. I repeat it again: You are at liberty to make any possible Supposition: And you may destroy one Supposition by another: But then you may not retain the Consequences, or any part of the Consequences of your first Supposition so destroyed. I admit that Signs may be made to denote either any thing or nothing: And consequently that in the original Notation $x + o$, o might have signified either an Increment or nothing. But then which of these soever you make it signify, you must argue consistently with such its Signification, and not proceed upon a double Meaning: which to do were a manifest Sophism. Whether you argue in Symbols or in Words, the Rules of right Reason are still the same. Nor can it be supposed, you will plead a Privilege in Mathematics to be exempt from them.

XVI. If you assume at first a Quantity increased by nothing, and in the Expression $x + o$, o stands for nothing, upon this Supposition as there is no Increment of the Root, so there will be no Increment of the Power; and consequently there will be none except the first, of all those Members of the Series constituting the Power of the Binomial; you will therefore never come at your Expression of a Fluxion legitimately by such Method. Hence you are driven into the fallacious way of proceeding to a certain Point on the Supposition of an Increment, and then at once shifting your Supposition to that of no Increment. There may seem great Skill in doing this at a certain Point or Period. Since if this second Supposition had been made before the common Division by o, all had vanished at once, and you must have got nothing by your Supposition. Whereas by this Artifice of first dividing, and then changing your Supposition, you retain I and nx^{n-1}. But, notwithstanding all this address to cover it, the fallacy is still the same. For whether it be done sooner or later, when once the second Supposition or Assumption is made, in the same instant the former Assumption and all that you got by it is destroyed, and goes out together. And this is universally true, be the Subject what it will, throughout all the Branches of humane Knowledge; in any other of which, I believe, Men would hardly admit such a reasoning as this, which in Mathematics is accepted for Demonstration.

XVII. It may not be amiss to observe, that the Method for finding the Fluxion of a Rectangle of two flowing Quantities, as it is set forth in the Treatise of Quadratures, differs from the abovementioned taken from the second Book of the Principles, and is in effect the same with that used in the *calculus differentialis*. [NOTE: Analyse des Infiniment Petits, part I. prop. 2.] For the supposing a Quantity infinitely diminished and therefore rejecting it, is in effect the rejecting an Infinitesimal; and indeed it requires a marvellous sharpness of Discernment, to be able to distinguish between evanescent Increments and infinitesimal Differences. It may perhaps be said that the Quantity being infinitely diminished becomes nothing, and so nothing is rejected. But according to the received Principles it is evident, that no Geometrical Quantity, can by any division or subdivision whatsoever be exhausted, or reduced to nothing. Considering the various Arts and Devices used by the great author of the Fluxionary Method: in how many Lights he placeth his Fluxions: and in what different ways he attempts to demonstrate the same Point: one would be inclined to think, he was himself suspicious of the justness of his own demonstrations; and that he was not enough pleased with any one notion steadily to adhere to it. Thus much at least is plain, that he owned himself satisfied concerning certain Points, which nevertheless he could not undertake to demonstrate to others. [NOTE: *See Letter to Collins, Nov. 8, 1676.*] Whether this satisfaction arose from tentative Methods or Inductions; which have often been admitted by Mathematicians (for instance by Dr. *Wallis* in his Arithmetic of Infinites) is what I shall not pretend to determine. But, whatever the Case might have been with respect to the Author, it appears that his Followers have shewn themselves more eager in applying his Method, than accurate in examining his Principles.

XVIII. It is curious to observe, what subtilty and skill this great Genius employs to struggle with an insuperable Difficulty; and through what Labyrinths he endeavours to escape the Doctrine of Infinitesimals; which as it intrudes upon him whether he will or no, so it is admitted and embraced by others without the least repugnance. *Leibnitz* and his followers in their *calculus differentialis* making no manner of scruple, first to suppose, and secondly to reject Quantities infinitely small: with what clearness in the Apprehension and justness in the reasoning, any thinking Man, who is not prejudiced in favour of those things, may easily discern. The Notion or Idea of an infinitesimal Quantity, as it is an Object simply apprehended by the Mind, hath been already considered. [NOTE: *Sect. 5 and 6.*] I shall now only observe as to the method of getting rid of such Quantities, that it is done without the least Ceremony. As in Fluxions the Point of first importance, and which paves the way to the rest, is to find the Fluxion of a Product of two indeterminate Quantities, so in the *calculus differentialis* (which Method is supposed to have been borrowed from the former with some small Alterations) the main Point is to obtain the difference of such Product. Now the Rule for this is got by rejecting the Product or Rectangle of the Differences. And in general it is supposed, that no Quantity is bigger or lesser for the Addition or Subduction of its Infinitesimal: and that consequently no error can arise from such rejection of Infinitesimals.

XIX. And yet it should seem that, whatever errors are admitted in the Premises, proportional errors ought to be apprehended in the Conclusion, be they finite or infinitesimal: and that therefore the ἀκρίβεια of Geometry requires nothing should be neglected or rejected. In answer to this you will perhaps say, that the Conclusions are accurately true, and that therefore the Principles and Methods from whence they are derived must be so too. But this inverted way of demonstrating your Principles by your Conclusions, as it would be peculiar to you Gentlemen, so it is contrary to the Rules of Logic. The truth of the Conclusion will not prove either the Form or the Matter of a Syllogism to be true: inasmuch as the Illation might have been wrong or the Premises false, and the Conclusion nevertheless true, though not in virtue of such Illation or of such Premises. I say that in every other Science Men prove their Conclusions by their Principles, and not their Principles by the Conclusions. But if in yours you should allow your selves this unnatural way of proceeding, the Consequence would be that you must take up with Induction, and bid adieu to Demonstration. And if you submit to this, your Authority will no longer lead the way in Points of Reason and Science.

XX. I have no Controversy about your Conclusions, but only about your Logic and Method. How you demonstrate? What Objects you are conversant with, and whether you conceive them clearly? What Principles you proceed upon; how sound they may be; and how you apply them? It must be remembred that I am not concerned about the truth of your Theorems, but only about the way of coming at them; whether it be legitimate or illegitimate, clear or obscure, scientific or tentative. To prevent all possibility of your mistaking me, I beg leave to repeat and insist, that I consider the Geometrical Analyst as a Logician, *i. e.* so far forth as he reasons and argues; and his Mathematical Conclusions, not in themselves, but in their Premises; not as true or false, useful or insignificant, but as derived from such Principles, and by such Inferences. And forasmuch as it may perhaps seem an unaccountable Paradox, that Mathematicians should deduce true Propositions from false Principles, be right in the Conclusion, and yet err in the Premises; I shall endeavour particularly to explain why this may come to pass, and shew how Error may bring forth Truth, though it cannot bring forth Science.

XXI. In order therefore to clear up this Point, we will suppose for instance that a Tangent is to be drawn to a Parabola, and examine the progress of this Affair, as it is performed by infinitesimal Differences.

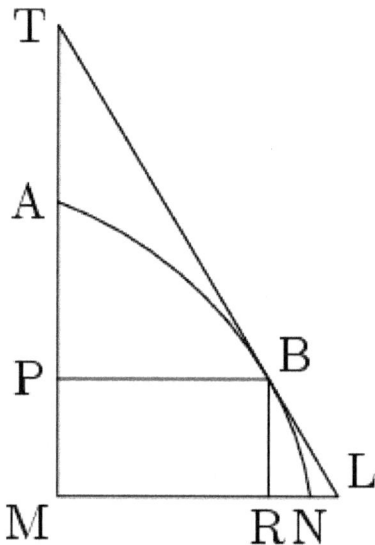

Let AB be a Curve, the Abscisse $AP = x$, the Ordinate $PB = y$, the Difference of the Abscisse $PM = dx$, the Difference of the Ordinate $RN = dy$. Now by supposing the Curve to be a Polygon, and consequently BN, the Increment or Difference of the Curve, to be a straight Line coincident with the Tangent, and the differential Triangle BRN to be similar to the triangle TPB

24

the Subtangent *PT* is found a fourth Proportional to *RN* : *RB* : *PB*: that is to *dy* : *dx* : *y*. Hence the Subtangent will be

$$\frac{y\,dx}{dy}.$$

But herein there is an error arising from the aforementioned false supposition, whence the value of *PT* comes out greater than the Truth: for in reality it is not the Triangle *RNB* but *RLB* which is similar to *PBT*, and therefore (instead of *RN*) *RL* should have been the first term of the Proportion, *i. e. RN* + *NL*, *i. e. dy* + *z*. whence the true expression for the Subtangent should have been

$$\frac{y\,dx}{dy+z}.$$

There was therefore an error of defect in making *dy* the divisor: which error was equal to *z*, *i. e. NL* the Line comprehended between the Curve and the Tangent. Now by the nature of the Curve *yy* = *px*, supposing *p* to be the Parameter, whence by the rule of Differences 2*y dy* = *p dx* and

$$dy = \frac{p\,dx}{2y}.$$

But if you multiply *y* + *dy* by it self, and retain the whole Product without rejecting the Square of the Difference, it will then come out, by substituting the augmented Quantities in the Equation of the Curve, that

$$dy = \frac{p\,dx}{2y} - \frac{dy\,dy}{2y}$$

truly. There was therefore an error of excess in making

$$dy = \frac{p\,dx}{2y},$$

which followed from the erroneous Rule of Differences. And the measure of this second error is

$$\frac{dy\,dy}{2y} = z.$$

Therefore the two errors being equal and contrary destroy each other; the first error of defect being corrected by a second error of excess.

XXII. If you had committed only one error, you would not have come at a true Solution of the Problem. But by virtue of a twofold mistake you arrive, though not at Science, yet at Truth. For Science it cannot be called, when you proceed blindfold, and arrive at the Truth not knowing how or by what means. To demonstrate that z is equal to

$$\frac{dy\,dy}{2y},$$

let *BR* or *dx* be *m* and *RN* or *dy* be *n*. By the thirty third Proposition of the first Book of the Conics of *Apollonius*, and from similar Triangles, as $2x$ to y so is *m* to

$$n + z = \frac{my}{2x}.$$

Likewise from the Nature of the Parabola $yy + 2yn + nn = xp + mp$, and $2yn + nn = mp$. wherefore

$$\frac{2yn + nn}{p} = m :$$

and because $yy = px$,

$$\frac{yy}{p}$$

will be equal to x. Therefore substituting these values instead of m and x we shall have

$$n + z = \frac{my}{2x} = \frac{2yynp + ynnp}{2yyp} :$$

i. e.

$$n + z = \frac{2yn + nn}{2y} :$$

which being reduced gives

$$z = \frac{nn}{2y} = \frac{dy\,dy}{2y} \qquad Q.E.D.$$

XXIII. Now I observe in the first place, that the Conclusion comes out right, not because the rejected Square of *dy* was infinitely small; but because this error was compensated by another contrary and equal error. I observe in the second place, that whatever is rejected, be it every so small, if it be real, and consequently makes a real error in the Premises, it will produce a proportional real error in the Conclusion. Your Theorems therefore cannot be accurately true, nor your Problems accurately solved, in virtue of Premises, which themselves are not accurate, it being a rule in Logic that *Conclusio sequitur partem debiliorem.*

Therefore I observe in the third place, that when the Conclusion is evident and the Premises obscure, or the Conclusion accurate and the Premises inaccurate, we may safely pronounce that such Conclusion is neither evident nor accurate, in virtue of those obscure inaccurate Premises or Principles; but in virtue of some other Principles which perhaps the Demonstrator himself never knew or thought of. I observe in the last place, that in case the Differences are supposed finite Quantities ever so great, the Conclusion will nevertheless come out the same: inasmuch as the rejected Quantities are legitimately thrown out, not for their smallness, but for another reason, to wit, because of contrary errors, which destroying each other do upon the whole cause that nothing is really, though something is apparently thrown out. And this Reason holds equally, with respect to Quantities finite as well as infinitesimal, great as well as small, a Foot or a Yard long as well as the minutest Increment.

XXIV. For the fuller illustration of this Point, I shall consider it in another light, and proceeding in finite Quantities to the Conclusion, I shall only then make use of one Infinitesimal.

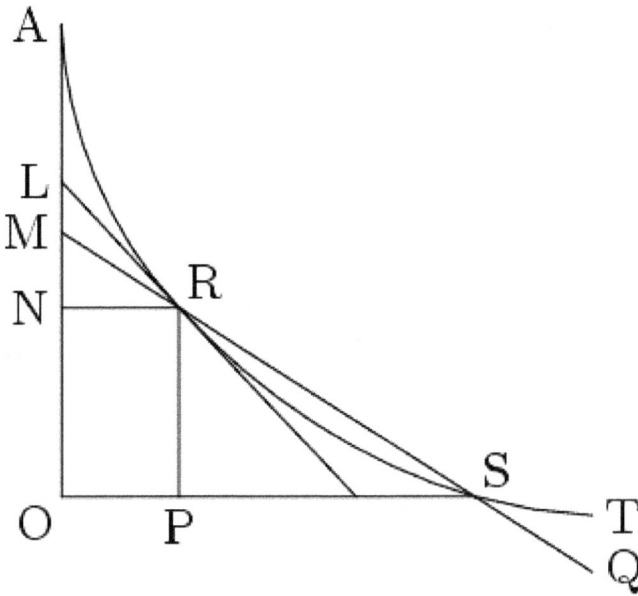

Suppose the straight Line *MQ* cuts the Curve *AT* in the points *R* and *S*. Suppose *LR* a Tangent at the Point *R*, *AN* the Abscisse, *NR* and *OS* Ordinates. Let *AN* be produced to *O*, and *RP* be drawn parallel to *NO*. Suppose *AN* = *x*, *NR* = *y*, *NO* = *v*, *PS* = *z*, the subsecant *MN* = *s*. Let the Equation *y* = *xx* express the nature of the Curve: and supposing *y* and *x* increased by their finite Increments, we get *y* + *z* = *xx* + *2xv* + *vv*. whence the former Equation being subducted there remains *z* = *2xv* + *vv*. And by reason of similar Triangles

$$PS : PR :: NR : NM, \quad i.\,e. \quad z : v :: y : s = \frac{vy}{z},$$

wherein if for *y* and *z* we substitute their values, we get

$$\frac{vxx}{2xv + vv} = s = \frac{xx}{2x + v}.$$

And supposing NO to be infinitely diminished, the subsecant NM will in that case coincide with the subtangent NL, and v as an Infinitesimal may be rejected, whence it follows that

$$s = NL = \frac{xx}{2x} = \frac{x}{2};$$

which is the true value of the Subtangent. And since this was obtained by one only error, *i. e.* by once rejecting one only Infinitesimal, it should seem, contrary to what hath been said, that an infinitesimal Quantity or Difference may be neglected or thrown away, and the Conclusion nevertheless be accurately true, although there was no double mistake or rectifying of one error by another, as in the first Case. But if this Point be thoroughly considered, we shall find there is even here a double mistake, and that one compensates or rectifies the other. For in the first place, it was supposed, that when NO is infinitely diminished or becomes an Infinitesimal, then the Subsecant NM becomes equal to the Subtangent NL. But this is a plain mistake, for it is evident, that as a Secant cannot be a Tangent, so a Subsecant cannot be a Subtangent. Be the Difference ever so small, yet still there is a Difference. And if NO be infinitely small, there will even then be an infinitely small Difference between NM and NL. Therefore NM or s was too little for your supposition, (when you supposed it equal to NL) and this error was compensated by a second error in throwing out v, which last error made s bigger than its true value, and in lieu thereof gave the value of the Subtangent. This is the true State of the Case, however it may be disguised. And to this in reality it amounts, and is at bottom the same thing, if we should pretend to find the Subtangent by having first found, from the Equation of the Curve and similar Triangles, a general Expression for all Subsecants, and then reducing the Subtangent under this general Rule, by considering it as the Subsecant when v vanishes or becomes nothing.

XXV. Upon the whole I observe, *First*, that *v* can never be nothing so long as there is a secant. *Secondly*, that the same Line cannot be both tangent and secant. *Thirdly*, that when *v* and *NO* [NOTE: *See the foregoing Figure.*] vanisheth, *PS* and *SR* do also vanish, and with them the proportionality of the similar Triangles. Consequently the whole Expression, which was obtained by means thereof and grounded thereupon, vanisheth when *v* vanisheth. *Fourthly*, that the Method for finding Secants or the Expression of Secants, be it ever so general, cannot in common sense extend any further than to all Secants whatsoever: and, as it necessarily supposeth similar Triangles, it cannot be supposed to take place where there are not similar Triangles. *Fifthly*, that the Subsecant will always be less than the Subtangent, and can never coincide with it; which Coincidence to suppose would be absurd; for it would be supposing, the same Line at the same time to cut and not to cut another given Line, which is a manifest Contradiction, such as subverts the Hypothesis and gives a Demonstration of its Falshood. *Sixthly*, if this be not admitted, I demand a Reason why any other apagogical Demonstration, or Demonstration *ad absurdum* should be admitted in Geometry rather than this: Or that some real Difference be assigned between this and others as such. *Seventhly*, I observe that it is sophistical to suppose *NO* or *RP*, *PS*, and *SR* to be finite real Lines in order to form the Triangle *RPS*, in order to obtain Proportions by similar Triangles; and afterwards to suppose there are no such Lines, nor consequently similar Triangles, and nevertheless to retain the Consequence of the first Supposition, after such Supposition hath been destroyed by a contrary one. *Eighthly*, That although, in the present case, by inconsistent Suppositions Truth may be obtained, yet that such Truth is not demonstrated: That such Method is not conformable to the Rules of Logic and right Reason: That, however useful it may be, it must be considered only as a Presumption, as a Knack, an Art, rather an Artifice, but not a scientific Demonstration.

XXVI. The Doctrine premised may be farther illustrated by the following simple and easy Case, wherein I shall proceed by evanescent Increments.

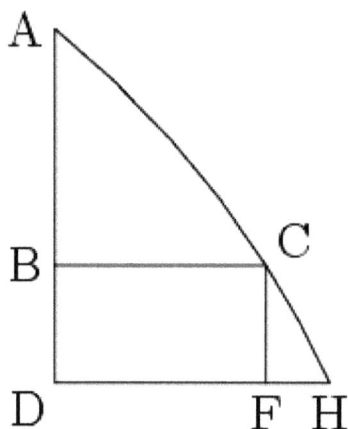

Suppose $AB = x$, $BC = y$, $BD = o$, and that xx is equal to the Area ABC. It is proposed to find the Ordinate y or BC. When x by flowing becomes $x + o$, then xx becomes $xx + 2xo + oo$. And the Area ABC becomes ADH, and the Increment of xx will be equal to $BDHC$ the Increment of the Area, $i.\ e.$ to $BCFD + CFH$. And if we suppose the curvilinear Space CFH to be qoo, then $2xo + oo = yo + qoo$, which divided by o give $2x + o = y + qo$. And, supposing o to vanish, $2x = y$, in which Case ACH will be a straight Line, and the Areas ABC, CFH, Triangles. Now with regard to this Reasoning, it hath been already remarked, [NOTE: $Sect.$ 12 and 13. supra.] that it is not legitimate or logical to suppose o to vanish, $i.\ e.$ to be nothing, $i.\ e.$ that there is no Increment, unless we reject at the same time with the Increment it self every Consequence of such Increment, $i.\ e.$ whatsoever could not be obtained but by supposing such Increment. It must nevertheless be acknowledged, that the Problem is rightly solved, and the Conclusion true, to which we are led by this Method. It will therefore be asked, how comes it to pass that the throwing out o is attended with no Error in the Conclusion? I answer, the true reason hereof is plainly this: Because q being Unite, qo is equal to o. And therefore $2x + o - qo = y = 2x$, the equal Quantities qo and o being destroyed by contrary Signs.

XXVII. As on the one hand it were absurd to get rid of o by saying, let me contradict my self: Let me subvert my own Hypothesis: Let me take it for granted that there is no Increment, at the same time that I retain a Quantity, which I could never have got at but by assuming an Increment: So on the other hand it would be equally wrong to imagine, that in a geometrical Demonstration we may be allowed to admit any Error, though ever so small, or that it is possible, in the nature of Things, an accurate Conclusion should be derived from inaccurate Principles. Therefore o cannot be thrown out as an Infinitesimal, or upon the Principle that Infinitesimals may be safely neglected. But only because it is destroyed by an equal Quantity with a negative Sign, whence $o - qo$ is equal to nothing. And as it is illegitimate to reduce an Equation, by subducting from one Side a Quantity when it is not to be destroyed, or when an equal Quantity is not subducted from the other Side of the Equation: So it must be allowed a very logical and just Method of arguing, to conclude that if from Equals either nothing or equal Quantities are subducted, they shall still remain equal. And this is a true Reason why no Error is at last produced by the rejecting of o. Which therefore must not be ascribed to the Doctrine of Differences, or Infinitesimals, or evanescent Quantities, or Momentums, or Fluxions.

XXVIII. Suppose the Case to be general, and that x^n is equal to the Area ABC, whence by the Method of Fluxions the Ordinate is found nx^{n-1} which we admit for true, and shall inquire how it is arrived at. Now if we are content to come at the Conclusion in a summary way, by supposing that the Ratio of the Fluxions of x and x^n are found [NOTE: *Sect.* 13.] to be I and nx^{n-1}, and that the Ordinate of the Area is considered as its Fluxion; we shall not so clearly see our way, or perceive how the truth comes out, that Method as we have shewed before being obscure and illogical. But

33

if we fairly delineate the Area and its Increment, and divide the latter into two Parts *BCFD* and *CFH*, [NOTE: *See the Figure in Sect. 26.*] and proceed regularly by Equations between the algebraical and geometrical Quantities, the reason of the thing will plainly appear. For as x^n is equal to the Area *ABC*, so is the Increment of x^n equal to the Increment of the Area, *i. e.* to *BDHC*; that is, to say,

$$nox^{n-1} + \frac{nn - n}{2} oox^{n-2} + \&c. = BDFC + CFH.$$

And only the first Members, on each Side of the Equation being retained, $nox^{n-1} = BDFC$: and dividing both Sides by o or *BD*, we shall get $nx^{n-1} = $ BC. Admitting, therefore, that the curvilinear Space *CFH* is equal to the rejectaneous Quantity

$$\frac{nn - n}{2} oox^{n-2} + \&c.$$

and that when this is rejected on one Side, that is rejected on the other, the Reasoning becomes just and the Conclusion true. And it is all one whatever Magnitude you allow to *BD*, whether that of an infinitesimal Difference or a finite Increment ever so great. It is therefore plain, that the supposing the rejectaneous algebraical Quantity to be an infinitely small or evanescent Quantity, and therefore to be neglected, must have produced an Error, had it not been for the curvilinear Spaces being equal thereto, and at the same Time subducted from the other Part or Side of the Equation agreeably to the Axiom, *If from Equals you subduct Equals, the Remainders will be equal.* For those Quantities which by the Analysts are said to be neglected, or made to vanish, are in reality subducted. If therefore the Conclusion be true, it is absolutely necessary that the finite Space *CFH* be equal to the Remainder of the Increment expressed by

$$\frac{nn-n}{2}oox^{n-2} \quad \mathcal{E}c.$$

equal I say to the finite Remainder of a finite Increment.

XXIX. Therefore, be the Power what you please, there will arise on one Side an algebraical Expression, on the other a geometrical Quantity, each of which naturally divides it self into three Members: The algebraical or fluxionary Expression, into one which includes neither the Expression of the Increment of the Absciss nor of any Power thereof, another which includes the Expression of the Increment it self, and the third including the Expression of the Powers of the Increment. The geometrical Quantity also or whole increased Area consists of three Parts or Members, the first of which is the given Area, the second a Rectangle under the Ordinate and the Increment of the Absciss, and the third a curvilinear Space. And, comparing the homologous or correspondent Members on both Sides, we find that as the first Member of the Expression is the Expression of the given Area, so the second Member of the Expression will express the Rectangle or second Member of the geometrical Quantity; and the third, containing the Powers of the Increment, will express the curvilinear Space, or third Member of the geometrical Quantity. This hint may, perhaps, be further extended and applied to good purpose, by those who have leisure and curiosity for such Matters. The use I make of it is to shew, that the Analysis cannot obtain in Augments or Differences, but it must also obtain in finite Quantities, be they ever so great, as was before observed.

XXX. It seems therefore upon the whole that we may safely pronounce, the Conclusion cannot be right, if in order thereto any Quantity be made to vanish, or be neglected, except that either one Error is redressed by another; or that secondly, on the same Side of an Equation equal Quantities are destroyed by contrary Signs, so that the Quantity we mean to reject is first annihilated; or lastly, that from opposite Sides equal Quantities are subducted. And therefore to get rid of Quantities by the received Principles of Fluxions or of Differences is neither good Geometry nor good Logic. When the Augments vanish, the Velocities also vanish. The Velocities or Fluxions are said to be *primò* and *ultimò*, as the Augments nascent and evanescent. Take therefore the *Ratio* of the evanescent Quantities, it is the same with that of the Fluxions. It will therefore answer all Intents as well. Why then are Fluxions introduced? Is it not to shun or rather to palliate the Use of Quantities infinitely small? But we have no Notion whereby to conceive and measure various Degrees of Velocity, besides Space and Time, or when the Times are given, besides Space alone. We have even no Notion of Velocity prescinded from Time and Space. When therefore a Point is supposed to move in given Times, we have no Notion of greater or lesser Velocities or of Proportions between Velocities, but only of longer and shorter Lines, and of Proportions between such Lines generated in equal Parts of Time.

XXXI. A Point may be the limit of a Line: A Line may be the limit of a Surface: A Moment may terminate Time. But how can we conceive a Velocity by the help of such Limits? It necessarily implies both Time and Space, and cannot be conceived without them. And if the Velocities of nascent and evanescent Quantities, *i. e.* abstracted from Time and Space, may not be comprehended, how can we comprehend and demonstrate their Proportions? Or consider their *rationes primae* and *ultimae?* For to consider the Proportion or *Ratio* of Things implies that such Things have Magnitude: That such their Magnitudes may be measured, and their Relations to each other known. But, as there is no measure of Velocity except Time and Space, the Proportion of Velocities being only compounded of the direct Proportion of the Spaces, and the reciprocal Proportion of the Times; doth it not follow that to talk of investigating, obtaining, and considering the Proportions of Velocities, exclusively of Time and Space, is to talk unintelligibly?

XXXII. But you will say that, in the use and application of Fluxions, men do not overstrain their Faculties to a precise Conception of the abovementioned Velocities, Increments, Infinitesimals, or any other such like Ideas of a Nature so nice, subtile, and evanescent. And therefore you will perhaps maintain, that Problems may be solved without those inconceivable Suppositions: and that, consequently, the Doctrine of Fluxions, as to the practical Part, stands clear of all such Difficulties. I answer, that if in the use or application of this Method, those difficult and obscure Points are not attended to, they are nevertheless supposed. They are the Foundations on which the Moderns build, the Principles on which they proceed, in solving Problems and discovering Theorems. It is with the Method of Fluxions as with all other Methods, which presuppose their respective Principles and are grounded thereon. Although the rules may be practised by Men who neither attend to, nor perhaps know the Principles. In like manner, therefore, as a Sailor may practically apply certain Rules derived from Astronomy and Geometry, the Principles whereof he doth not understand: And as any ordinary Man may solve divers numerical Questions, by the vulgar Rules and Operations of Arithmetic, which he performs and applies without knowing the Reasons of them: Even so it cannot be denied that you may apply the Rules of the fluxionary Method: You may compare and reduce particular Cases to general Forms: You may operate and compute and solve Problems thereby, not only without an actual Attention to, or an actual Knowledge of, the Grounds of that Method, and the Principles whereon it depends, and whence it is deduced, but even without having ever considered or comprehended them.

XXXIII. But then it must be remembred, that in such Case although you may pass for an Artist, Computist, or Analyst, yet you may not be justly esteemed a Man of Science and Demonstration. Nor should any Man, in virtue of being conversant in such obscure Analytics, imagine his rational Faculties to be more improved than those of other Men, which have been exercised in a different manner, and on different Subjects; much less erect himself into a Judge and an Oracle, concerning Matters that have no sort of connexion with, or dependence on those Species, Symbols or Signs, in the Management whereof he is so conversant and expert. As you, who are a skilful Computist or Analyst, may not therefore be deemed skilful in Anatomy: or *vice versa*, as a Man who can dissect with Art, may, nevertheless, be ignorant in your Art of computing: even so you may both, notwithstanding your peculiar Skill in your respective Arts, be alike unqualified to decide upon Logic, or Metaphysics, or Ethics, or Religion. And this would be true, even admitting that you understood your own Principles and could demonstrate them.

XXXIV. If it is said, that Fluxions may be expounded or expressed by finite Lines proportional to them: Which finite Lines, as they may be distinctly conceived and known and reasoned upon, so they may be substituted for the Fluxions, and their mutual Relations or Proportions be considered as the Proportions of Fluxions: By which means the Doctrine becomes clear and useful. I answer that if, in order to arrive at these finite Lines proportional to the Fluxions, there be certain Steps made use of which are obscure and inconceivable, be those finite lines themselves ever so clearly conceived, it must nevertheless be acknowledged, that your proceeding is not clear nor your method scientific.

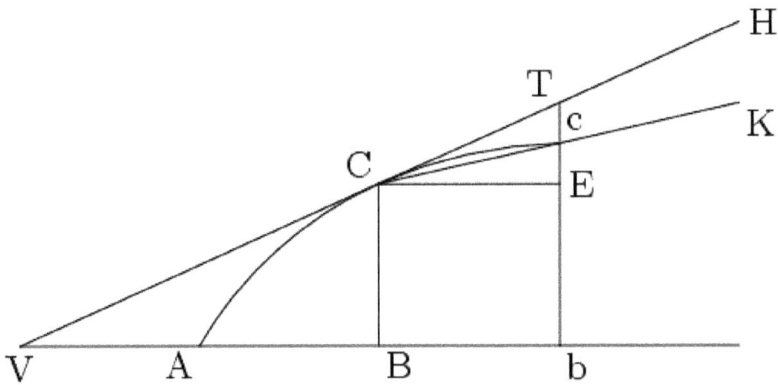

For instance, it is supposed that *AB* being the Absciss, *BC* the Ordinate, and *VCH* a Tangent of the Curve *AC*, *Bb* or *CE* the Increment of the Absciss, *Ec* the Increment of the Ordinate, which produced meets *VH* in the Point *T*, and *Cc* the Increment of the Curve. The right Line *Cc* being produced to *K*, there are formed three small Triangles, the Rectilinear *CEc*, the Mixtilinear *CEc*, and the Rectilinear Triangle *CET*. It is evident these three Triangles are different from each other, the Rectilinear *CEc* being less than the Mixtilinear *CEc*, whose Sides are the three Increments abovementioned, and this still less than the Triangle *CET*. It is supposed that the Ordinate *bc* moves into the place *BC*, so that the Point *c* is coincident with the Point *C*; and the right Line *CK*, and consequently the Curve *Cc*, is coincident with the Tangent *CH*. In which case the mixtilinear evanescent Triangle *CEc* will, in its last form, be similar to the Triangle *CET*: And its evanescent Sides *CE*, *Ec* and *Cc* will be proportional to *CE*, *ET* and *CT* the Sides of the Triangle *CET*. And therefore it is concluded, that the Fluxions of the lines *AB*, *BC*, and *AC*, being in the last Ratio of their evanescent Increments, are proportional to the Sides of the Triangle *CET*, or, which is all one, of the Triangle *VBC* similar thereunto. [NOTE: Introd. ad Quad. Curv.] It is particularly remarked and insisted on by the great Author, that the Points *C* and *c* must not be distant one from another, by any the least Interval whatsoever: But that, in order to find the ultimate Proportions of the Lines

CE, *Ec*, and *Cc* (*i. e.* the Proportions of the Fluxions or Velocities) expressed by the finite Sides of the Triangle *VBC*, the Points *C* and *c* must be accurately coincident, *i. e.* one and the same. A Point therefore is considered as a Triangle, or a Triangle is supposed to be formed in a Point. Which to conceive seems quite impossible. Yet some there are, who, though they shrink at all other Mysteries, make no difficulty of their own, who strain at a Gnat and swallow a Camel.

XXXV. I know not whether it be worth while to observe, that possibly some Men may hope to operate by Symbols and Suppositions, in such sort as to avoid the use of Fluxions, Momentums, and Infinitesimals after the following manner. Suppose x to be one Absciss of a Curve, and z another Absciss of the same Curve. Suppose also that the respective Areas are xxx and zzz: and that $z - x$ is the Increment of the Absciss, and $zzz - xxx$ the Increment of the Area, without considering how great, or how small those Increments may be. Divide now $zzz - xxx$ by $z - x$ and the Quotient will be $zz + zx + xx$: and, supposing that z and x are equal, this same Quotient will be $3xx$ which in that case is the Ordinate, which therefore may be thus obtained independently of Fluxions and Infinitesimals. But herein is a direct Fallacy: for in the first place, it is supposed that the Abscisses z and x are unequal, without such supposition no one step could have been made; and in the second place, it is supposed they are equal; which is a manifest Inconsistency, and amounts to the same thing that hath been before considered. [NOTE: *Sect.* 15.] And there is indeed reason to apprehend, that all Attempts for setting the abstruse and fine Geometry on a right Foundation, and avoiding the Doctrine of Velocities, Momentums, &c. will be found impracticable, till such time as the Object and the End of Geometry are better understood, than hitherto they seem to have been. The great Author of the Method of Fluxions felt this Difficulty, and therefore he gave in to those nice Abstractions and Geometrical Metaphysics, without which he saw nothing could be done on the received Principles; and what in the way of

Demonstration he hath done with them the Reader will judge. It must, indeed, be acknowledged, that he used Fluxions, like the Scaffold of a building, as things to be laid aside or got rid of, as soon as finite Lines were found proportional to them. But then these finite Exponents are found by the help of Fluxions. Whatever therefore is got by such Exponents and Proportions is to be ascribed to Fluxions: which must therefore be previously understood. And what are these Fluxions? The Velocities of evanescent Increments? And what are these same evanescent Increments? They are neither finite Quantities nor Quantities infinitely small, nor yet nothing. May we not call them the Ghosts of departed Quantities?

XXXVI. Men too often impose on themselves and others, as if they conceived and understood things expressed by Signs, when in truth they have no Idea, save only of the very Signs themselves. And there are some grounds to apprehend that this may be the present Case. The Velocities of evanescent or nascent Quantities are supposed to be expressed, both by finite Lines of a determinate Magnitude, and by Algebraical Notes or Signs: but I suspect that many who, perhaps never having examined the matter, take it for granted, would upon a narrow scrutiny find it impossible, to frame any Idea or Notion whatsoever of those Velocities, exclusive of such finite Quantities and Signs.

Suppose the line *KP* described by the Motion of a Point continually accelerated, and that in equal Particles of time the unequal Parts *KL*, *LM*, *MN*, *NO*, &c. are generated. Suppose also that *a*, *b*, *c*, *d*, *e*, &c. denote the Velocities of the generating Point, at the several Periods of the Parts or Increments so generated. It is easy to observe that these Increments are each proportional to the sum of the Velocities with which it is described: That, consequently, the several Sums of the Velocities, generated in equal Parts of Time, may be set forth by the respective Lines *KL, LM, MN, &c.* generated in the same Times: It is likewise an easy matter to say, that the last Velocity generated in the first Particle of Time, may be expressed by the Symbol *a*, the last in the second by *b*, the last generated in the third by *c*, and so on: that *a* is the Velocity of *LM* in *statu nascenti*, and *b*, *c*, *d*, *e*, *&c.* are the Velocities of the Increments *MN, NO, OP, &c.* in their respective nascent estates. You may proceed, and consider these Velocities themselves as flowing or increasing Quantities, taking the Velocities of the Velocities, and the Velocities of the Velocities of the Velocities, *i. e.* the first, second, third *&c.* Velocities *ad infinitum*: which succeeding Series of Velocities may be thus expressed, *a. b - a. c - 2b + a. d - 3c + 3b - a. &c.* which you may call by the names of the first, second, third, fourth Fluxions. And for an apter Expression you may denote the variable flowing Line *KL, KM, KN, &c.* by the Letter *x*; and the first Fluxions by $\dot{x}$, the second by $\ddot{x}$, the third by $\dddot{x}$, and so on *ad infinitum*.

XXXVII. Nothing is easier than to assign Names, Signs, or Expressions to these Fluxions, and it is not difficult to compute and operate by means of such Signs. But it will be found much more difficult, to omit the Signs and yet retain in our Minds the things, which we suppose to be signified by them. To consider the Exponents, whether Geometrical, or Algebraical, or Fluxionary, is no difficult Matter. But to form a precise Idea of a third Velocity for instance, in it self and by it self, *Hoc opus, hic labor.* Nor indeed is it an easy point, to form a clear and distinct Idea of any Velocity at all, exclusive of and prescinding from all length of time and space; as also from all Notes, Signs, or Symbols whatsoever. This, if I may be allowed to judge of others by my self, is impossible. To me it seems evident, that Measures and Signs are absolutely necessary, in order to conceive or reason about Velocities; and that, consequently, when we think to conceive the Velocities, simply and in themselves, we are deluded by vain Abstractions.

XXXVIII. It may perhaps be thought by some an easier Method of conceiving Fluxions, to suppose them the Velocities wherewith the infinitesimal Differences are generated. So that the first Fluxions shall be the Velocities of the first Differences, the second the Velocities of the second Differences, the third Fluxions the Velocities of the third Differences, and so on *ad infinitum*. But not to mention the insurmountable difficulty of admitting or conceiving Infinitesimals, and Infinitesimals of Infinitesimals, &c. it is evident that this notion of Fluxions would not consist with the great Author's view; who held that the minutest Quantity ought not to be neglected, that therefore the Doctrine of Infinitesimal Differences was not to be admitted in Geometry, and who plainly appears to have introduced the use of Velocities or Fluxions, on purpose to exclude or do without them.

XXXIX. To others it may possibly seem, that we should form a juster Idea of Fluxions by assuming the finite unequal isochronal Increments *KL, LM, MN*, &c. and considering them in *statu nascenti*, also their Increments in *statu nascenti*, and the nascent Increments of those Increments, and so on, supposing the first nascent Increments to be proportional to the first Fluxions or Velocities, the nascent Increments of those Increments to be proportional to the second Fluxions, the third nascent Increments to be proportional to the third Fluxions, and so onwards. And, as the first Fluxions are the Velocities of the first nascent Increments, so the second Fluxions may be conceived to be the Velocities of the second nascent Increments, rather than the Velocities of Velocities. But which means the Analogy of Fluxions may seem better preserved, and the notion rendered more intelligible.

XL. And indeed it should seem, that in the way of obtaining the second or third Fluxion of an Equation, the given Fluxions were considered rather as Increments than Velocities. But the considering them sometimes in one Sense, sometimes in another, one while in themselves, another in their Exponents, seems to have occasioned no small share of that Confusion and Obscurity, which is found in the Doctrine of Fluxions. It may seem therefore, that the Notion might be still mended, and that instead of Fluxions of Fluxions, or Fluxions of Fluxions of Fluxions, and instead of second, third, or fourth, &c. Fluxions of a given Quantity, it might be more consistent and less liable to exception to say, the Fluxion of the first nascent Increment, *i. e.* the second Fluxion; the Fluxion of the second nascent Increment *i. e.* the third Fluxion; the Fluxion of the third nascent Increment, *i. e.* the fourth Fluxion, which Fluxions are conceived respectively proportional, each to the nascent Principle of the Increment succeeding that whereof it is the Fluxion.

XLI. For the more distinct Conception of all which it may be considered, that if the finite Increment *LM* [NOTE: *See the foregoing Scheme in Sect.* 36.] be divided into the Isochronal Parts *Lm, mn, no, oM;* and the Increment *MN* divided into the Parts *Mp, pq, qr, rN* Isochronal to the former; as the whole Increments *LM, MN* are proportional to the Sums of their describing Velocities, even so the homologous Particles *Lm, Mp* are also proportional to the respective accelerated Velocities with which they are described. And as the Velocity with which *Mp* is generated, exceeds that with which *Lm* was generated, even so the Particle *Mp* exceeds the Particle *Lm.* And in general, as the Isochronal Velocities describing the Particles of *MN* exceed the Isochronal Velocities describing the Particles of *LM,* even so the Particles of the former exceed the correspondent Particles of the latter. And this will hold, be the said Particles ever so small. *MN* therefore will exceed *LM* if they are both taken in their nascent States: and that excess will be proportional to the excess of the Velocity *b* above the Velocity *a.* Hence we may see that this last account of Fluxions comes, in the upshot, to the same thing with the first. [NOTE: *Sect.* 36.]

XLII. But notwithstanding what hath been said it must still be acknowledged, that the finite Particles *Lm* or *Mp*, though taken ever so small, are not proportional to the Velocities *a* and *b*; but each to a Series of Velocities changing every Moment, or which is the same thing, to an accelerated Velocity, by which it is generated, during a certain minute Particle of time: That the nascent beginnings or evanescent endings of finite Quantities, which are produced in Moments or infinitely small Parts of Time, are alone proportional to given Velocities: That, therefore, in order to conceive the first Fluxions, we must conceive Time divided into Moments, Increments generated in those Moments, and Velocities proportional to those Increments: That in order to conceive second and third Fluxions, we must suppose that the nascent Principles or momentaneous Increments have themselves also other momentaneous Increments, which are proportional to their respective generating Velocities: That the Velocities of these second momentaneous Increments are second Fluxions: those of their nascent momentaneous Increments third Fluxions. And so on *ad infinitum*.

XLIII. By subducting the Increment generated in the first Moment from that generated in the second, we get the Increment of an Increment. And by subducting the Velocity generating in the first Moment from that generating in the second, we get the Fluxion of a Fluxion. In like manner, by subducting the Difference of the Velocities generating in the two first Moments, from the excess of the Velocity in the third above that in the second Moment, we obtain the third Fluxion. And after the same Analogy we may proceed to fourth, fifth, sixth Fluxions &c. And if we call the Velocities of the first, second, third, fourth Moments, *a, b, c, d,* the Series of Fluxions will be as above, *a. b - a. c - 2b + a. d - 3c + 3b - a. ad infinitum, i. e. $\dot{x}$. $\ddot{x}$. $\dddot{x}$. $\ddddot{x}$. ad infinitum.*

XLIV. Thus Fluxions may be considered in sundry Lights and Shapes, which seem all equally difficult to conceive. And indeed, as it is impossible to conceive Velocity without time or space, without either finite length or finite Duration, [NOTE: *Sect.* 31.] it must seem above the powers of Men to comprehend even the first Fluxions. And if the first are incomprehensible, what shall we say of the second and third Fluxions, *&c.*? He who can conceive the beginning of a beginning, or the end of an end, somewhat before the first or after the last, may be perhaps sharpsighted enough to conceive these things. But most Men will, I believe, find it impossible to understand them in any sense whatever.

XLV. One would think that Men could not speak too exactly on so nice a Subject. And yet, as was before hinted, we may often observe that the Exponents of Fluxions or Notes representing Fluxions are confounded with the Fluxions themselves. Is not this the Case, when just after the Fluxions of flowing Quantities were said to be the Celerities of their increasing, and the second Fluxions to be the mutations of the first Fluxions or Celerities, we are told that $\overset{\prime\prime}{z}.\ \overset{\prime}{z}.\ z.\ \dot{z}.\ \ddot{z}.\ \overset{..}{\dot{z}}.$[NOTE: De Quadratura Curvarum.] represents a Series of Quantities, whereof each subsequent Quantity is the Fluxion of the preceding; and each foregoing is a fluent Quantity having the following one for its Fluxion?

XLVI. Divers Series of Quantities and Expressions, Geometrical and Algebraical, may be easily conceived, in Lines, in Surfaces, in Species, to be continued without end or limit. But it will not be found so easy to conceive a Series, either of mere Velocities or of mere nascent Increments, distinct therefrom and corresponding thereunto. Some perhaps may be led to think the Author intended a Series of Ordinates, wherein each Ordinate was the Fluxion of the preceding and Fluent of the following, *i. e.* that the Fluxion of one Ordinate was it self the Ordinate of another Curve; and the Fluxion of this last Ordinate was the Ordinate of yet another Curve; and so on *ad infinitum.* But who can conceive how the Fluxion (whether Velocity or nascent Increment) of an Ordinate should be it self an Ordinate? Or more than that each preceding

Quantity or Fluent is related to its Subsequent or Fluxion, as the Area of a curvilinear Figure to its Ordinate; agreeably to what the Author remarks, that each preceding Quantity in such Series is as the Area of a curvilinear Figure, whereof the Absciss is z, and the Ordinate is the following Quantity.

XLVII. Upon the whole it appears that the Celerities are dismissed, and instead thereof Areas and Ordinates are introduced. But however expedient such Analogies or such Expressions may be found for facilitating the modern Quadratures, yet we shall not find any light given us thereby into the original real nature of Fluxions; or that we are enabled to frame from thence just Ideas of Fluxions considered in themselves. In all this the general ultimate drift of the Author is very clear, but his Principles are obscure. But perhaps those Theories of the great Author are not minutely considered or canvassed by his Disciples; who seem eager, as was before hinted, rather to operate than to know, rather to apply his Rules and his Forms, than to understand his Principles and enter into his Notions. It is nevertheless certain, that in order to follow him in his Quadratures, they must find Fluents from Fluxions; and in order to this, they must know to find Fluxions from Fluents; and in order to find Fluxions, they must first know what Fluxions are. Otherwise they proceed without Clearness and without Science. Thus the direct Method precedes the inverse, and the knowledge of the Principles is supposed in both. But as for operating according to Rules, and by the help of general Forms, whereof the original Principles and Reasons are not understood, this is to be esteemed merely technical. Be the Principles therefore ever so abstruse and metaphysical, they must be studied by whoever would comprehend the Doctrine of Fluxions. Nor can any Geometrician have a right to apply the Rules of the great Author, without first considering his metaphysical Notions whence they were derived. These how necessary soever in order to Science, which can never be obtained without a precise, clear, and accurate Conception of the Principles, are nevertheless by several carelessly passed over; while the Expressions alone are dwelt on and considered and treated with great Skill and Management, thence to obtain other Expressions by Methods, suspicious and indirect (to say the least) if considered in themselves, however recommended by Induction and Authority; two Motives which are acknowledged sufficient to beget a rational Faith and moral Persuasion, but nothing higher.

XLVIII. You may possibly hope to evade the Force of all that hath been said, and to screen false Principles and inconsistent Reasonings, by a general Pretence that these Objections and Remarks are Metaphysical. But this is a vain Pretence. For the plain Sense and Truth of what is advanced in the foregoing Remarks, I appeal to the Understanding of every unprejudiced intelligent Reader. To the same I appeal, whether the Points remarked upon are not most incomprehensible Metaphysics. And Metaphysics not of mine, but your own. I would not be understood to infer, that your Notions are false or vain because they are Metaphysical. Nothing is either true or false for that Reason. Whether a Point be called Metaphysical or no avails little. The Question is whether it be clear or obscure, right or wrong, well or ill-deduced?

XLIX. Although momentaneous Increments, nascent and evanescent Quantities, Fluxions and Infinitesimals of all Degrees, are in truth such shadowy Entities, so difficult to imagine or conceive distinctly, that (to say the least) they cannot be admitted as Principles or Objects of clear and accurate Science: and although this obscurity and incomprehensibility of your Metaphysics had been alone sufficient, to allay your Pretensions to Evidence; yet it hath, if I mistake not, been further shewn, that your Inferences are no more just than your Conceptions are clear, and that your Logics are as exceptionable as your Metaphysics. It should seem therefore upon the whole, that your Conclusions are not attained by just Reasoning from clear Principles; consequently that the Employment of modern Analysts, however useful in mathematical Calculations, and Constructions, doth not habituate and qualify the Mind to apprehend clearly and infer justly; and consequently, that you have no right in Virtue of such Habits, to dictate out of your proper Sphere, beyond which your Judgment is to pass for no more than that of other Men.

L. Of a long Time I have suspected, that these modern Analytics were not scientifical, and gave some Hints thereof to the Public about twenty five Years ago. Since which time, I have been diverted by other Occupations, and imagined I might employ my self better than in deducing and laying together my Thoughts on so nice a Subject. And though of late I have been called upon to make good my Suggestions; yet, as the Person, who made this Call, doth not appear to think maturely enough to understand, either those Metaphysics which he would refute, or Mathematics which he would patronize, I should have spared my self the trouble of writing for his Conviction. Nor should I now have troubled you or my self with this Address, after so long an Intermission of these Studies; were it not to prevent, so far as I am able, your imposing on your self and others in Matters of much higher Moment and Concern. And to the end that you may more clearly comprehend the Force and Design of the foregoing Remarks, and pursue them still further in your own Meditations, I shall subjoin the following Queries.

Query I. Whether the Object of Geometry be not the Proportions of assignable Extensions? And whether, there be any need of considering Quantities either infinitely great or infinitely small?

Qu. 2. Whether the end of Geometry be not to measure assignable finite Extension? And whether this practical View did not first put Men on the study of Geometry?

Qu. 3. Whether the mistaking the Object and End of Geometry hath not created needless Difficulties, and wrong Pursuits in that Science?

Qu. 4. Whether Men may properly be said to proceed in a scientific Method, without clearly conceiving the Object they are conversant about, the End proposed, and the Method by which it is pursued?

Qu. 5. Whether it doth not suffice, that every assignable number of Parts may be contained in some assignable Magnitude? And whether it be not unnecessary, as well as absurd, to suppose that finite Extension is infinitely divisible?

Qu. 6. Whether the Diagrams in a Geometrical Demonstration are not to be considered, as Signs of all possible finite Figures, of all sensible and imaginable Extensions or Magnitudes of the same kind?

Qu. 7. Whether it be possible to free Geometry from insuperable Difficulties and Absurdities, so long as either the abstract general Idea of Extension, or absolute external Extension be supposed its true Object?

Qu. 8. Whether the Notions of absolute Time, absolute Place, and absolute Motion be not most abstractedly Metaphysical? Whether it be possible for us to measure, compute, or know them?

Qu. 9. Whether Mathematicians do not engage themselves in Disputes and Paradoxes, concerning what they neither do nor can conceive? And whether the Doctrine of Forces be not a sufficient Proof of this? [NOTE: See a *Latin* treatise, *De Motu*, published at *London*, in the year 1721.]

Qu. 10. Whether in Geometry it may not suffice to consider assignable finite Magnitude, without concerning our selves with Infinity? And whether it would not be righter to measure large Polygons having finite Sides, instead of Curves, than to suppose Curves are Polygons of infinitesimal Sides, a Supposition neither true nor conceivable?

Qu. 11. Whether many Points, which are not readily assented to, are not nevertheless true? And whether those in the two following Queries may not be of that Number?

Qu. 12. Whether it be possible, that we should have had an Idea or Notion of Extension prior to Motion? Or whether if a Man had never perceived Motion, he would ever have known or conceived one thing to be distant from another?

Qu. 13. Whether Geometrical Quantity hath coexistent Parts? And whether all Quantity be not in a flux as well as Time and Motion?

Qu. 14. Whether Extension can be supposed an Attribute of a Being immutable and eternal?

Qu. 15. Whether to decline examining the Principles, and unravelling the Methods used in Mathematics, would not shew a bigotry in Mathematicians?

Qu. 16. Whether certain Maxims do not pass current among Analysts, which are shocking to good Sense? And whether the common Assumption that a finite Quantity divided by nothing is infinite be not of this Number?

Qu. 17. Whether the considering Geometrical Diagrams absolutely or in themselves, rather than as Representatives of all assignable Magnitudes or Figures of the same kind, be not a principal Cause of the supposing finite Extension infinitely divisible; and of all the Difficulties and Absurdities consequent thereupon?

Qu. 18. Whether from Geometrical Propositions being general, and the Lines in Diagrams being therefore general Substitutes or Representatives, it doth not follow that we may not limit or consider the number of Parts, into which such particular Lines are divisible?

Qu. 19. When it is said or implied, that such a certain Line delineated on Paper contains more than any assignable number of Parts, whether any more in truth ought to be understood, than that it is a Sign indifferently representing all finite Lines, be they ever so great. In which relative Capacity it contains, *i. e.* stands for more than any assignable number of Parts? And whether it be not altogether absurd to suppose a finite Line, considered in it self or in its own positive Nature, should contain an infinite number of Parts?

Qu. 20. Whether all Arguments for the infinite Divisibility of finite Extension do not suppose and imply, either general abstract Ideas or absolute external Extension to be the Object of Geometry? And, therefore, whether, along with those Suppositions, such Arguments also do not cease and vanish?

Qu. 21. Whether the supposed infinite Divisibility of finite Extension hath not been a Snare to Mathematicians, and a Thorn in their Sides? And whether a Quantity infinitely diminished and a Quantity infinitely small are not the same thing?

Qu. 22. Whether it be necessary to consider Velocities of nascent or evanescent Quantities, or Moments, or Infinitesimals? And whether the introducing of Things so inconceivable be not a reproach to Mathematics?

Qu. 23. Whether Inconsistencies can be Truths? Whether Points repugnant and absurd are to be admitted upon any Subject, or in any Science? And whether the use of Infinites ought to be allowed, as a sufficient Pretext and Apology, for the admitting of such Points in Geometry?

Qu. 24. Whether a Quantity be not properly said to be known, when we know its Proportion to given Quantities? And whether this Proportion can be known, but by Expressions or Exponents, either Geometrical, Algebraical, or Arithmetical? And whether Expressions in Lines or Species can be useful but so far forth as they are reducible to Numbers?

Qu. 25. Whether the finding out proper Expressions or Notations of Quantity be not the most general Character and Tendency of the Mathematics? And Arithmetical Operation that which limits and defines their Use?

Qu. 26. Whether Mathematicians have sufficiently considered the Analogy and Use of Signs? And how far the specific limited Nature of things corresponds thereto?

Qu. 27. Whether because, in stating a general Case of pure Algebra, we are at full liberty to make a Character denote, either a positive or a negative Quantity, or nothing at all, we may therefore in a geometrical Case, limited by Hypotheses and Reasonings from particular Properties and Relations of Figures, claim the same Licence?

Qu. 28. Whether the Shifting of the Hypothesis, or (as we may call it) the *fallacia Suppositionis* be not a Sophism, that far and wide infects the modern Reasonings, both in the mechanical Philosophy and in the abstruse and fine Geometry?

Qu. 29. Whether we can form an Idea or Notion of Velocity distinct from and exclusive of its Measures, as we can of Heat distinct from and exclusive of the Degrees on the Thermometer, by which it is measured? And whether this be not supposed in the Reasonings of modern Analysts?

Qu. 30. Whether Motion can be conceived in a Point of Space? And if Motion cannot, whether Velocity can? And if not, whether a first or last Velocity can be conceived in a mere Limit, either initial or final, of the described Space?

Qu. 31. Where there are no Increments, whether there can be any *Ratio* of Increments? Whether Nothings can be considered as proportional to real Quantities? Or whether to talk of their Proportions be not to talk Nonsense? Also in what Sense we are to understand the Proportion of a Surface to a Line, of an Area to an Ordinate? And whether Species or Numbers, though properly expressing Quantities which are not homogeneous, may yet be said to express their Proportion to each other?

Qu. 32. Whether if all assignable Circles may be squared, the Circle is not, to all intents and purposes, squared as well as the Parabola? Of whether a parabolical Area can in fact be measured more accurately than a Circular?

Qu. 33. Whether it would not be righter to approximate fairly, than to endeavour at Accuracy by Sophisms?

Qu. 34. Whether it would not be more decent to proceed by Trials and Inductions, than to pretend to demonstrate by false Principles?

Qu. 35. Whether there be not a way of arriving at Truth, although the Principles are not scientific, nor the Reasoning just? And whether such a way ought to be called a Knack or a Science?

Qu. 36. Whether there can be Science of the Conclusion, where there is not Evidence of the Principles? And whether a Man can have Evidence of the Principles, without understanding them? And therefore, whether the Mathematicians of the present Age act like Men of Science, in taking so much more pains to apply their Principles, than to understand them?

Qu. 37. Whether the greatest Genius wrestling with false Principles may not be foiled? And whether accurate Quadratures can be obtained without new *Postulata* or Assumptions? And if not, whether those which are intelligible and consistent ought not to be preferred to the contrary? *See* Sect. XXVIII *and* XXIX.

Qu. 38. Whether tedious Calculations in Algebra and Fluxions be the likeliest Method to improve the Mind? And whether Mens being accustomed to reason altogether about Mathematical Signs and Figures, doth not make them at a loss how to reason without them?

Qu. 39. Whether, whatever readiness Analysts acquire in stating a Problem, or finding apt Expressions for Mathematical Quantities, the same doth necessarily infer a proportionable ability in conceiving and expressing other Matters?

Qu. 40. Whether it be not a general Case or Rule, that one and the same Coefficient dividing equal Products gives equal Quotients? And yet whether such Coefficient can be interpreted by o or nothing? Or whether any one will say, that if the Equation $2 \times o = 5 \times o$, be divided by o, the Quotients on both Sides are equal? Whether therefore a Case may not be general with respect to all Quantities, and yet not extend to Nothings, or include the Case of Nothing? And whether the bringing Nothing under the notion of Quantity may not have betrayed Men into false Reasoning?

Qu. 41. Whether in the most general Reasonings about Equalities and Proportions, Men may not demonstrate as well as in Geometry? Whether in such Demonstrations, they are not obliged to the same strict Reasoning as in Geometry? And whether such their Reasonings are not deduced from the same Axioms with those in Geometry? Whether therefore Algebra be not as truly a Science as Geometry?

Qu. 42. Whether Men may not reason in Species as well as in Words? Whether the same Rules of Logic do not obtain in both Cases? And whether we have not a right to expect and demand the same Evidence in both?

Qu. 43. Whether an Algebraist, Fluxionist, Geometrician, or Demonstrator of any kind can expect indulgence for obscure Principles or incorrect Reasonings? And whether an Algebraical Note or Species can at the end of a Process be interpreted in a Sense, which could not have been substituted for it at the beginning? Or whether any particular Supposition can come under a general Case which doth not consist with the reasoning thereof?

Qu. 44. Whether the Difference between a mere Computer and a Man of Science be not, that the one computes on Principles clearly conceived, and by Rules evidently demonstrated, whereas the other doth not?

Qu. 45. Whether, although Geometry be a Science, and Algebra allowed to be a Science, and the Analytical a most excellent Method, in the Application nevertheless of the Analysis to Geometry, Men may not have admitted false Principles and wrong Methods of Reasoning?

Qu. 46. Whether, although Algebraical Reasonings are admitted to be ever so just, when confined to Signs or Species as general Representatives of Quantity, you may not nevertheless fall into Error, if, when you limit them to stand for particular things, you do not limit your self to reason consistently with the Nature of such particular things? And whether such Error ought to be imputed to pure Algebra?

Qu. 47. Whether the View of modern Mathematicians doth not rather seem to be the coming at an Expression by Artifice, than at the coming at Science by Demonstration?

Qu. 48. Whether there may not be sound Metaphysics as well as unsound? Sound as well as unsound Logic? And whether the modern Analytics may not be brought under one of these Denominations, and which?

Qu. 49. Whether there be not really a *Philosophia prima*, a certain transcendental Science superior to and more extensive than Mathematics, which it might behove our modern Analysts rather to learn than despise?

Qu. 50. Whether ever since the recovery of Mathematical Learning, there have not been perpetual Disputes and Controversies among the Mathematicians? And whether this doth not disparage the Evidence of their Methods?

Qu. 51. Whether any thing but Metaphysics and Logic can open the Eyes of Mathematicians and extricate them out of their Difficulties?

Qu. 52. Whether upon the received Principles a Quantity can by any Division or Subdivision, though carried ever so far, be reduced to nothing?

Qu. 53. Whether if the end of Geometry be Practice, and this Practice be Measuring, and we measure only assignable Extensions, it will not follow that unlimited Approximations completely answer the Intention of Geometry?

Qu. 54. Whether the same things which are now done by Infinites may not be done by finite Quantities? And whether this would not be a great Relief to the Imaginations and Understandings of Mathematical Men?

Qu. 55. Whether those Philomathematical Physicians, Anatomists, and Dealers in the Animal Oeconomy, who admit the Doctrine of Fluxions with an implicit Faith, can with a good grace insult other Men for believing what they do not comprehend?

Qu. 56. Whether the Corpuscularian, Experimental, and Mathematical Philosophy so much cultivated in the last Age, hath not too much engrossed Mens Attention; some part whereof it might have usefully employed?

Qu. 57. Whether from this, and other concurring Causes, the Minds of speculative Men have not been borne downward, to the debasing and stupifying of the higher Faculties? And whether we may not hence account for that prevailing Narrowness and Bigotry among many who pass for Men of Science, their Incapacity for things Moral, Intellectual, or Theological, their Proneness to measure all Truths by Sense and Experience of animal Life?

Qu. 58. Whether it be really an Effect of Thinking, that the same Men admire the great Author for his Fluxions, and deride him for his Religion?

Qu. 59. If certain Philosophical Virtuosi of the present Age have no Religion, whether it can be said to be for want of Faith?

Qu. 60. Whether it be not a juster way of reasoning, to recommend Points of Faith from their Effects, than to demonstrate Mathematical Principles by their Conclusions?

Qu. 61. Whether it be not less exceptionable to admit Points above Reason than contrary to Reason?

Qu. 62. Whether Mysteries may not with better right be allowed of in Divine Faith, than in Humane Science?

Qu. 63. Whether such Mathematicians as cry out against Mysteries, have ever examined their own Principles?

Qu. 64. Whether Mathematicians, who are so delicate in religious Points, are strictly scrupulous in their own Science? Whether they do not submit to Authority, take things upon Trust, and believe Points inconceivable? Whether they have not their Mysteries, and what is more, their Repugnancies and Contradictions?

Qu. 65. Whether it might not become Men, who are puzzled and perplexed about their own Principles, to judge warily, candidly, and modestly concerning other Matters?

Qu. 66. Whether the modern Analytics do not furnish a strong *argumentum ad hominem* against the Philomathematical Infidels of these Times?

Qu. 67. Whether it follows from the abovementioned Remarks, that accurate and just Reasoning is the peculiar Character of the present Age? And whether the modern Growth of Infidelity can be ascribed to a Distinction so truly valuable?

www.ingramcontent.com/pod-product-compliance
Lightning Source LLC
Chambersburg PA
CBHW071750090426
42738CB00011B/2633